Are Drug Asset Forfeiture Laws Corrupting the Police?

Research on Public Policy Series

STEWART J. D'ALESSIO

LISA STOLZENBERG

JAMIE L. FLEXON

Cover art supplied by Kevin KAL Kallaugher,

The Economist, Kaltoons.com

CONTENTS

CONTENTS

1 EXECUTIVE SUMMARY

Drug asset forfeiture laws allow the government to seize the cash and property of citizens as a means to help diminish illicit drug consumption among the population and the violence often associated with the drug trade. These laws have an added benefit in that they afford law enforcement agencies the ability to supplement their budgets with the cash and property seized from drug offenders. The income derived from drug asset forfeiture seizures is a major revenue source for law enforcement, generating approximately 100 million for police agencies in 2010. Estimates indicate that about 20 percent of a police department's budget is derived from drug asset forfeiture proceeds (Coe and Wiesel, 2001). The police not only generate a considerable amount of income from drug asset forfeiture seizures, but many police administrators claim that they are financially dependent on this money to fund the day-to-day operations of their department (Williams, 2002).

Although the primary purpose of drug asset forfeiture laws is to decrease criminal activity, it is widely believed that the pragmatic organizational exigency of income generation, coupled with broad police discretion in the enforcement of drug laws (Alexander, 2012), is supplanting the more abstract and difficult to quantify goal of legal legitimacy in the arrest sanction. To illustrate, a national survey conducted in January of 2015 found that 38 percent of American adults believe that drug asset forfeiture laws are motivating the police to make legally questionable drug arrests in order to seize people's cash and property.[1]

The purpose of this study is to determine empirically whether drug asset forfeiture laws are actually having a deleterious effect on drug enforcement. If drug asset forfeiture laws are compelling the police to make legally suspect drug arrests as many people believe, the likelihood of conviction for a felony drug offense should be substantially lower in counties where the police derive a greater amount of income from drug

[1] The national survey of 800 likely voters was conducted by Pulse Opinion Re-search on January 6-7, 2015. Pulse Opinion Research, LLC is an independent public opinion research firm using automated polling methodology and procedures licensed from Rasmussen Reports, LLC. The margin of sampling error is +/- 3.5 percentage points with a 95 percent level of confidence.

asset forfeiture seizures. This is a reasonable supposition as the determination of guilt in a criminal case is a rough indicator of the degree that the police are conforming to the law during the performance of their duties. Thus, controlling for non-drug convictions and other factors related to the likelihood of conviction, there should be a substantive negative relationship between the amount of income the police earn from drug asset forfeiture seizures and the likelihood that a felony drug defendant will be convicted for his or her crime.

Figure 1 graphically depicts the aggregate relationship between the income the police earn from drug asset forfeiture seizures and the percent of drug cases that result in a felony conviction for 37 large U.S. counties in 2000. In contrast to what many people believe, a visual examination of this figure readily shows little association between drug asset forfeiture income and the percent of felony drug cases that result in a criminal conviction. Such a finding suggests at least tentatively that legally unwarranted drug arrests are not substantially more pervasive in counties where the police earn a higher income from drug asset forfeiture seizures.

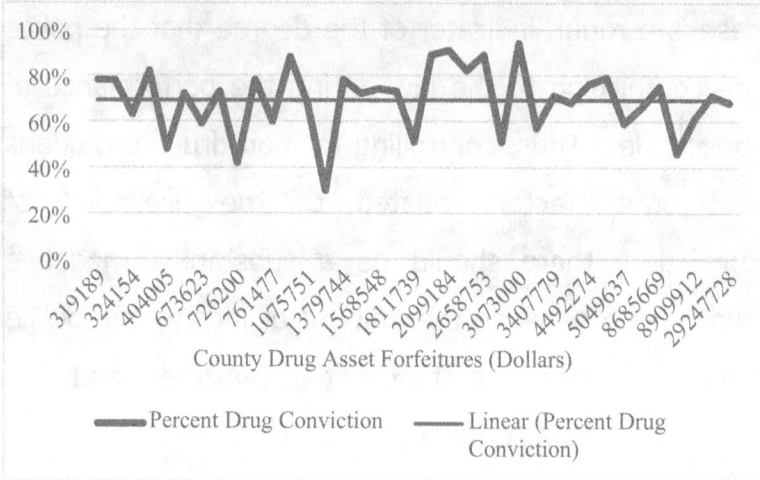

Figure 1. Percent Drug Conviction by the Drug Asset Forfeitures in 37 U.S. Counties

The results generated in a more sophisticated multilevel analysis add additional support to the data displayed in Figure 1 by showing that the likelihood of conviction for a felony drug crime is not substantially lower in counties where the police derive a greater amount of income from drug asset forfeiture seizures, controlling for a number of county-level and defendant-level variables. The likelihood of conviction is also not statistically different for black and white felony drug defendants in counties where the police generate more income from drug asset forfeiture seizures. In fact, there is no evidence of racial disparity in the likelihood of drug conviction generally because a black felony drug defendant has about the same odds of being convicted as a white felony drug defendant. This finding is interesting as it suggests that the police are not performing their drug enforcement duties in a racially biased manner.

In conclusion, despite the widespread belief that drug asset forfeiture laws are corrupting the police, this study finds no credible evidence that the supplemental income the police procure from drug asset forfeiture seizures is influencing them to effectuate drug arrests that are ultimately determined by the judicial system to be legally questionable.

2 SOCIAL AND INDIVIDUAL COST OF ILLICIT DRUG USE

An estimated 149 to 271 million people worldwide use illicit drugs (Degenhardt and Hall, 2012). Data culled from the National Survey on Drug Use and Health show that 22.5 million Americans over the age of 12, which is nearly nine percent of the U.S. population, used an illicit substance during the month prior to their being surveyed in 2011 (Substance Abuse and Mental Health Services Administration, 2012). The individual and social burdens associated with this illicit drug use are enormous, reportedly costing Americans about $193 billion dollars in 2007 alone (National Drug Intelligence Center, 2011). This monetary figure encompasses health care costs, lost productivity and criminal activity. Included in the public health care costs are expenditures for drug treatment, those needing acute care at emergency rooms and hospitals, insurance costs, and public costs for indigent and low-income persons (National Drug Intelligence Center, 2011). Unlike other social health issues, the use of illicit drugs also results in additional systemic costs because illegal drug use carries criminal penalties and the concomitant resources provided by state and federal criminal justice agencies (National Drug Intelligence Center, 2011).

Illicit drug use also has a number of adverse health related consequences for the individual. Research suggests a strong connection between illicit drug use, particular to injectables, and commutable diseases such as HIV/AIDS. Overdose mortality, suicides and traumas are also associated with amphetamines, opioids and cocaine (Degenhardt and Hall, 2012). Although cannabis, the most widely used illegal substance, is not correlated with increased mortality, an association exists between its use and mental disorders such as psychosis and schizophrenia (Lynskeya and Stranga, 2013). Illicit drug use also attenuates productivity due to the loss in gainful employment resulting from drug treatment, illness or imprisonment. These individual harms are not borne equally across social strata, as minorities are more apt to be subjected to them (Degenhardt and Hall, 2012).

3 FIGHTING THE WAR ON DRUGS

To address the problem of illicit drug use, President Nixon declared a War on Drugs in 1971.[2] It is estimated that this War on Drugs costs U.S. taxpayers over $51 billion annually (Drug Policy Alliance, 2013).[3] A variety of supply-side strategies are currently employed by the U.S. government in this war, including source control, interdiction, drug task forces, and mandatory penalties for drug crimes. Supply-side strategies attempt to diminish drug consumption in the general population by raising the price of illegal drugs. Supply control measures can influence the price of a drug in a number of different ways. For example, drug seizures may compel drug producers to increase the sale price of their drugs to recoup lost revenues. Drug producers may also raise the price of their drugs to cover the costs associated with asset seizure and to offset the potential threat of arrest and imprisonment. Finally, drug manufacturers may implement costly

---

[2] The War on Drugs in America has a long history dating back to the early 1900s (Robinson and Scherlen, 2007).
[3] Despite the billions spent by U.S. government, over 65 percent of Americans believe that the War on Drugs has been a failure in reducing the illegal drug trade (Angus Reid Public Opinion, 2012).

avoidance measures to circumvent the supply control activities of law enforcement (Moore, 1990). Supply-side strategies are thought to be effective in reducing drug consumption because users of illegal substances, particularly heavy users who interact with the criminal justice system, adjust their intake levels as drug prices fluctuate (Stolzenberg and D'Alessio, 2003).

Drug asset forfeiture laws are another weapon used by the government in its battle against drugs. Drug asset forfeiture laws seek to make the drug trade a less lucrative and more dangerous endeavor by disrupting the working capital of criminal organizations and by elevating the severity of an offender's punishment (Cassella, 2013). Although sometimes criticized on constitutional grounds (Kim, 1997), drug asset forfeiture laws enable the government to seize money and or property from an individual if the property is considered contraband, if illegal activities led to the acquisition of the property, if criminal activity was facilitated in some way by the property, and if a nexus exists between the property and a criminal enterprise (Edgeworth, 2009). Additionally, if a defendant has squandered or hidden assets related to a criminal offense, federal law enables the government to seize as a substitute other property of the defendant or impose a monetary judgment against the defendant to recoup the loss (Finneran and Luther, 2013).

Forfeiture can occur within a criminal or civil proceeding depending on the particular circumstances of the case (Kim, 1997). The government initiates a criminal forfeiture or in personam forfeiture after the conviction of the criminal defendant. An individual's property cannot be seized by the government unless there is an adjudication of guilt. Forfeiture in this context acts as an added element of a defendant's sentence. The standard constitutional due process rights that are afforded a defendant in his or her criminal case, such as proof of guilt beyond a reasonable doubt, are required in a criminal forfeiture proceeding.

In a civil forfeiture or in rem forfeiture, by contrast, the state focuses specifically on the tainted property rather than on the individual. This shift in focus permits the state to confiscate an individual's property without an adjudication of guilt. There are also fewer due process protections afforded a defendant in a civil forfeiture proceeding. For example, while "beyond a reasonable doubt" is the threshold of evidence needed to seize a person's assets in a criminal case, the lower threshold of "preponderance of the evidence" is only needed in a civil asset forfeiture proceeding. Although often criticized on constitutional grounds (Rosenberg, 1988), civil forfeitures are deemed essential to enhance the state's ability to recover any laundered proceeds derived from criminal activity (Cassella, 2008).

While the primary goal of drug asset forfeiture laws is to diminish illicit drug consumption and the violence associated with the drug trade, these laws have an added benefit of enabling law enforcement agencies to supplement their budgets with the cash and property seized from drug offenders. Drug asset forfeiture is a major source of extra revenue for police agencies, generating about 100 million for police agencies in 2010. About 20 percent of a police department's budget is comprised of drug asset forfeiture income (Coe and Wiesel, 2001). Police departments not only generate a considerable amount of supplemental income from drug asset forfeiture seizures, but surveys of police administrators show that many police departments have become dependent on this income to fund their daily operations (Blumenson and Nilsen, 1998; Williams, 2002).[4]

While the primary goal of drug asset forfeiture laws is to curtail drug related crime by making the trafficking and sale of narcotics a less lucrative endeavor, many remain convinced that the generation of supplemental income from drug asset forfeiture seizures has become an overriding organizational imperative that is motivating the police to focus on drug enforcement at the expense of enforcing other crimes including violent crimes. The work of Rothman (2002) and Weber (1978) may help to provide theoretical framework for understanding the logic of this viewpoint. These theorists proffer that the philosophical principles that provide the initial impetus and the underlying rationale for an institutional reform frequently conflict with the immediate, pragmatic

---

[4] This perceived dependency is somewhat exaggerated because the police are able to adequately perform their duties on a tight budget (Grosskopf et al., 1995).

objectives of the organization. Over time, the abstract philosophical principles that form the groundwork for a reform are supplanted by "policies and activities ... [that] maximize the rewards and minimize the strains for the organization" (Chambliss and Seidman, 1971:266). This *cooptation* manifests itself through the process of reform, conflict and displacement and is known as the *dialectic of conscience and convenience* (Rothman, 2002) or the *routinization of charisma* (Weber, 1978). Thus, many believe that the immediate, quantifiable and pragmatic goal of supplemental income generation,[5] while originally conceived as an ancillary goal of drug asset forfeiture laws, has usurped the primary goal of reducing illicit drug use and the crime associated with illegal drugs.

Furthermore, while the income derived from drug asset forfeiture seizures cannot be used for personal gain, it can still furnish indirect benefits for both police administrators and for rank-and-file police officers. It is often argued that public-sector organizations have

---

[5] Donation programs often provide an additional revenue source for police departments. However, in contrast to drug asset forfeiture, changes in law enforcement practices cannot influence the amount of income generated from donation programs (Stellwagen and Wylie, 1985).

an endemic tendency to expand in size (Downs, 1967). Within this framework, government officials are seen as "...empire-builders, imperialistically or avariciously intent upon maximizing the power or wealth of their offices and institutions" (Levinson, 2005:915). While public sector bureaucrats cannot maximize profit like their counterparts in private industry, they can still reap numerous personal benefits by expanding the size and budget of their agency. The benefits acquired from such expansion include increased status and power, a rise in personal income, greater opportunities for career advancement, and an enhanced ability of the agency to secure government subsidies. Even the rank-and-file of a public-sector organization benefit individually from a large budget since it helps to enhance career opportunities for advancement within the organization (Niskanen, 1991).

Prior research suggests support for the view that the lure of drug asset forfeiture income is motivating the police to overly direct their energies on drug enforcement. Studies find that law enforcement activities rather than the prevalence of drug trafficking and drug use are responsible for city variation in the number of drug arrests made by police (King, 2008; Mast et al., 2000). Police departments also appear to place a greater emphasis on drug control when they can keep a higher percentage of the proceeds seized in drug asset forfeitures (Baicker and Jacobson, 2007). The amount of income generated by the police from drug asset forfeiture not only increases as traditional funding to police agencies decreases, but the escalation in drug asset forfeiture income is particularly evident during periods of economic distress when traditional funding sources are evaporating (Baicker and Jacobson, 2007). Some even question whether drug asset forfeiture laws, as currently used, are having the anticipated deterrent effect (Johnson and Miceli, 2013).

Of course, any potentially corrupting influence of drug asset forfeiture income can easily be remedied by simply disallowing the police agency to retain the assets that it seized. However, while denying a police agency access to the income derived from its drug forfeiture activities appears to be a simplistic solution, police agencies will likely oppose any attempt to deny them the income generated from their drug enforcement efforts. Additionally, when one considers that state and local budget authorities frequently reduce appropriations in response to the amount of income generated by the police in asset seizures (Baicker and Jacobson, 2007), it stands to reason that politicians will be less than enthusiastic in curtailing the police's incentive to seize the cash and property of drug offenders as any shortfall in drug asset forfeiture income will likely have to be offset by an increase in traditional funding allocations.

4 SUMMARY

The primary purpose of this study is to determine whether drug asset forfeiture laws are having a harmful effect on drug enforcement because of the police's monetary incentive to *maximize financial recoveries* by making drug arrests (Lemos and Minzner, 2014). This monetary inducement, coupled with the discretion police officers exercise in the enforcement of drug laws (Alexander, 2012), has engendered the widespread belief that the police are probably making legally questionable drug arrests in order to seize people's cash and property. By legally questionable drug arrests, we mean drug arrests made by the police that fail to result in a criminal conviction.

The ultimate outcome of an arrest is an indirect indicator of the degree that the police are following the law when preforming their law enforcement duties. One of the strongest predictors in a prosecutor's decision to pursue a criminal case is the strength of evidence leveled against the defendant since a prosecutor's success is typically measured by his or her ability to secure convictions (Albonetti, 1987;

Eisenstein et al., 1999; Vera Institute of Justice, 1981). Prosecutors dismiss nearly half of all felony cases prior to a determination of guilt or innocence as a result of evidentiary or legal problems (Boland, 1983). Such a situation is commonplace for drug cases because of the potentially legally invalid search and seizure procedures employed by the police. To illustrate, a National Institute of Justice study found that while 4.8 percent of all felony arrests in the state of California were rejected by the prosecutor based on search and seizure problems, approximately 30 percent of the felony drug arrests made in two California prosecutor offices were rejected for similar reasons (Burkhart et al., 1982). It is readily apparent from this study that prosecutors feel that drug arrests are much more fraught with legal and evidentiary problems than arrests made by police for other types of crimes.

Using multilevel data drawn from 37 urbanized counties, we attempt to discern whether the amount of income the police derive from drug asset forfeiture seizures predicts the likelihood of conviction for a dug related felony offense, controlling for county-level and defendant-level factors typically predictive of criminal justice processing outcome. If the lure of financial gain is encouraging the police to make legally unwarranted drug arrests, the likelihood of conviction for a drug related felony offense should be substantially lower in counties where the police generate more money from drug asset forfeiture seizures.

A secondary objective of this study is to ascertain whether the race the defendant conditions the relationship between drug asset forfeiture income and the likelihood of a felony drug conviction. Addressing this issue has salience because black citizens have borne the brunt of the war waged on drugs. There were more than 25.4 million adult drug arrests in the U.S. between 1980 and 2007, with the black arrest rate being 2.8 to 5.5 times higher than the white arrest rate during this time-period (Human Rights Watch, 2009). This racial disparity in the drug arrest rate is speculated to result from the widespread perception among law enforcement that blacks have an enhanced proclivity to sell and use drugs (Gibbs, 1988). This negative view of black citizens as being the primary sellers and users of illegal drugs in the community is believed to compel the police to monitor and arrest them for drugs more frequently than is warranted based on their actual drug related criminal behavior (Beckett et al., 2005). It is also asserted that the police find it easier to target black drug dealers and users since they are more likely than whites to operate in public places (Goode, 2002; Saxe et al., 2001).

5 DATA AND ANALYSIS

This study analyzes data drawn from three different sources. These sources include the State Court Processing Statistics (SCPS) program dataset for criminal court processing information, the Law Enforcement Management and Administrative Statistics (LEMAS) dataset for forfeiture income information and the 2000 decennial census for environmental (county-level) information. The SCPS contains information on the prosecution of 118,556 felony criminal defendants in 65 of the 75 most populous counties in the United States in 2000 (Bureau of Justice Statistics, 2007).[6] This dataset contains information on the prosecution of felony cases filed in May of even numbered years. Each felony case prosecuted in state court is tracked until the final disposition of the case is reached, or until one year has passed since the filing of the case.

---

[6] A two-stage stratified sampling procedure, with the appropriate weighting of cases, was employed to collect the data. In the first-stage, a stratified sample was used to select the counties. In the second stage a systematic sample of felony filings within each selected county was drawn. The weight of each case is equal to the inverse probability of selection into the sample. These data are archived at the Inter-University Consortium for Political and Social Science Research at the University of Michigan.

Information relating to the demographic characteristics, arrest charges, criminal history, pretrial detention, adjudication, and sentencing outcome for each defendant is included in the dataset. The dataset is advantageous for our purposes because it contains information on each criminal case as it progresses through the criminal justice system, it has wide geographical breadth that allows for broad generalization of our results and it can be merged with other datasets aggregated at the county-level.

We merged the defendant-level data contained in the State Court Processing dataset with the LEMAS dataset and with the 2000 Census for 37 of the 65 counties.[7] The LEMAS survey is conducted every three to four years and contains information on over 3,000 state and local law enforcement agencies, including all those that employ 100 or more sworn officers and a nationally representative sample of smaller agencies. Data are obtained on the organization and administration of police and sheriffs' departments,

---

[7] We were able to match 37 counties in the State Court Processing dataset with the police department data contained in the LEMAS, but two counties were dropped from the multilevel analysis because of the lack of variation.

including agency responsibilities, operating expenditures, job functions of sworn and civilian employees, officer salaries and special pay, demographic characteristics of officers, weapons and armor policies, education and training requirements, computers and information systems, vehicles, special units, and community policing activities. We included several contextual variables drawn from the Census in the study because the social environment in which the police operate is thought to influence policing behavior (Eitle et al., 2005). The data are aggregated at the county-level as this is the smallest geographical unit for which the criminal court processing data are made available.

Dependent Variable

The dependent variable is a dichotomy indicating whether the drug defendant was convicted for his or her alleged crime. Convicted drug defendants are coded one. Non-convicted drug defendants are coded zero and include defendants who had their cases dropped by the prosecutor and defendants who failed to be convicted at trial.

Independent Variables

The defendant-level variables used to predict the likelihood of conviction include both extra-legal and legal variables commonly deemed salient in determining criminal justice processing outcome (Stolzenberg et al., 2013). Extra-legal variables include the defendant's race, age, gender, and type of defense attorney. The race of the defendant, which is the micro-level variable of theoretical interest, is coded one if the drug defendant is black and zero if white. Male drug defendants are coded one and female defendants zero. The age of the defendant is an interval variable. Moreover, because juveniles transferred to adult court are included in the dataset and since there is a possibility that these juveniles, along with elderly defendants, are treated more leniently, we model the effect of a defendant's age as a second order polynomial to ascertain whether a curvilinear relationship exists between age and the likelihood of drug conviction. If the relationship between the age of the defendant and the likelihood of conviction conforms to an inverted U-shaped pattern, the sign of the coefficient for the age variable will be positive and its square negative.

Defendants assigned a court-appointed attorney are coded one and zero if the defendant retained a private attorney. Previous research finds that private criminal lawyers enjoy a lower conviction rate than public defenders (Champion, 1989). The court appointed/private attorney variable also acts as a surrogate measure for a defendant's income level because a defendant's income and financial resources are predictive of whether a private attorney is retained (Gross, 2013). Controlling for a defendant's financial resources is relevant given that the majority of forfeiture cases involve modest homes and cars rather than the luxurious trappings often associated with the lifestyle of a successful drug lord (Schneider and Flaherty, 1991). For example, Carpenter and McGrath (2013) report that the average value of property seized in Georgia forfeiture cases was only $3,000 dollars. Low-level drug offenders are easy targets for forfeiture because they usually lack the financial resources to resist the overwhelming force of the government. The monetary costs associated with litigation coupled with attorneys' fees also frequently exceed the value of the asset(s) seized by the government making resistance a futile endeavor, notwithstanding whether the state had legitimate cause to seize the property.

The analysis also includes controls for several legally relevant variables. Prior criminal record is a composite measure of three variables, which include the number of prior felony convictions, the number of prior prison admissions and the number of prior misdemeanor convictions. Because preliminary analysis revealed excessive collinearity among the prior record variables, factor analysis was used to amalgamate them into a criminal history index.[8] Prior research suggests that a composite measure of prior criminal record has a stronger influence on severity of sanction than single-dimension indicators such as prior

---

[8] The principal component analysis of the three indicators of prior criminal record generated the following extraction and percent of variance scores: the number of prior felony convictions (.897, 65%), the number of prior prison admissions (.847, 25%) and the number of prior misdemeanor convictions (.658, 10%). The factor scores used to create the prior criminal record composite variable were calculated using the regression method.

convictions or prior incarcerations (Vigorita, 2001). A high score on this composite variable indicates that the drug defendant has a severe prior criminal record.

Other legally related factors taken into account in the analysis include whether the most serious charge involved the sale of drugs, the number of arrest charges filed against the defendant, whether the defendant was charged with a second felony, whether the defendant had an active criminal justice status at the time of the arrest, whether the defendant previously failed to appear in court, and whether the defendant was detained pretrial.

The macro-level variables included in the analysis were obtained from the LEMAS and from the 2000 Census. The macro-level variable of theoretical interest, which is derived from the LEMAS, is the amount of income measured in dollars (natural log) that the police in the county derived from drug asset forfeiture seizures. Because there are often multiple police departments in a single county and because any one of these police departments may have been responsible for a drug arrest, all the individual police departments in each of the counties were aggregated.

Nevertheless, the counties typically had one large police department that was responsible for the vast majority of the drug arrests and that generated the most income from drug asset forfeiture seizures. Table 1 ranks the 37 counties from high to low in reference to the amount of income derived from drug asset forfeiture seizures. Los Angeles County generated the most income from drug asset forfeiture seizures at slightly over 29 million dollars, whereas Santa Clara County generated the least amount of money at about 300,000 dollars. The average amount of drug asset forfeiture income generated by police in the 37 counties was 3,550,892 dollars.

Table 1. County Drug Asset Forfeitures

Santa Clara CA	$319,189
San Mateo CA	$320,780
Fairfax VA	$324,154
Contra Costa CA	$327,380
Baltimore (County) MD	$404,005
Macomb MI	$578,616
Pinellas FL	$673,623
Essex NJ	$713,567
Jefferson AL	$726,200
Salt Lake UT	$738,943
Philadelphia PA	$761,477
Montgomery MD	$789,800
Alameda CA	$1,075,751
Pima AZ	$1,179,027
San Bernardino CA	$1,379,744

New Haven CT	$1,520,079
Marion IN	$1,568,548
Honolulu HI	$1,746,175
Tarrant TX	$1,811,739
Franklin OH	$1,842,219
Westchester NY	$2,099,184
Dallas TX	$2,324,328
San Diego CA	$2,658,753
El Paso TX	$2,779,160
Nassau NY	$3,073,000
Fulton GA	$3,186,440
Orange CA	$3,407,779
Palm Beach FL	$3,928,703
Shelby TN	$4,492,274
Riverside CA	$4,759,699
Wayne MI	$5,049,637
Broward FL	$7,793,897
Travis TX	$8,685,669
Cook IL	$8,725,968
Maricopa AZ	$8,909,912
Harris TX	$11,459,880
Los Angeles CA	$29,247,728

SOURCE: U.S. Department of Justice. Bureau of Justice Statistics. Law Enforcement Management and Administrative Statistics (LEMAS): 2000 Sample Survey of Law Enforcement Agencies. ICPSR03565-v2. Ann Arbor, MI: Inter-university Consortium for Political and Social Research [distributor], 2008-12-04. http://doi.org/10.3886/ICPSR03565.v2

Several other contextual variables drawn from the 2000 Census are also incorporated into the analysis as statistical controls to avoid basing conclusions on spurious or suppressed relationships. These contextual variables include population density, percent male population 15-24 years of age, the crime rate, whether the county is situated in a southern state, percent non-drug convictions in the county, and community disadvantage. We also incorporate a percent black population variable and percent black population squared variable into the analysis to capture the possible curvilinear effect of racial threat. Although racial threat has been conceptualized in a variety of different ways (Eitle et al., 2002), Blalock (1967) argues in his power-threat hypothesis that as the size of the black population in a geographical location grows larger in size, whites increasingly perceive blacks as a threat to political ascendancy. This perceived threat in turn amplifies coercive efforts by the state to control the black population that may potentially become disruptive. However, Blalock maintains the relationship between racial threat and social control is curvilinear rather than linear. As the black population grows larger in size and racial threat becomes more acute, social control efforts employed by the state grow dramatically, suggesting an increasing slope associated with racial threat.

Finally, we include a composite variable derived from a principal components analysis of four indicators of community disadvantage: percent of the population (ages 25+) that never graduated from high school, percent households with public assistance income, percent female-headed households with children, and percent unemployed.[9] A higher score on this composite variable indicates a greater level of community disadvantage. We grand centered all the macro-level variables prior to their inclusion into the analysis. Table 2 shows the means, standard deviations and definitions for all the micro- and macro-level variables.

Table 2. Description of Variables Used in the Analysis

	Mean	Std. Dev.	Definition
Convicted	.71	.45	Coded 1 if defendant was convicted, 0 otherwise.
Defendant black	.61	.49	Coded 1 if defendant is black, 0 white.
Defendant male	.79	.41	Coded 1 if defendant is male,

---

[9] The principal components analysis of the four indicators of community disadvantage produced the following extraction and percent of variance scores: percent of the population (ages 25+) that never graduated from high school (.901, 75%), percent households with public assistance income (.873, 13%), percent female-headed households with children (.862, 8%), and percent unemployed (.835, 4%). The community disadvantage composite variable was created using the regression method.

	Mean	Std. Dev.	Definition
			0 female.
Active CJ status	.39	.49	Coded 1 if defendant had active criminal justice status when arrested, 0 otherwise.
Court-appointed attorney	.81	.39	Coded 1 if defendant received court-appointed attorney, 0 private attorney.
Prior FTA	.38	.49	Coded 1 if defendant had previously failed to appear for court appearance, 0 otherwise.
Second felony charge	.29	.45	Coded 1 if defendant was charged with second felony, 0 otherwise.
No. of charges	1.97	1.58	Total number of arrest charges.
Pretrial incarceration	.42	.49	Coded 1 if defendant was detained pretrial, 0 released pretrial.
Defendant's age	32.06	10.05	Defendant's age in years (centered and squared).
Drug sale	.45	.50	Coded 1 if most serious arrest charge involved drug sales, 0 drug possession or other drug-related charge.

	Mean	Std. Dev.	Definition
Criminal record	.00	1.00	Factor scores from principal component analysis of 3 variables: (a) # prior felony convictions, (b) # prior prison incarcerations, & (c) # prior misdemeanor convictions. Larger scores indicate more extensive criminal record.
Drug forfeitures	3,677,292.20	5,322,338.28	Drug asset forfeitures (dollars).
Percent non-drug convictions	57.82	17.90	Percent of non-drug prosecutions resulting in conviction.
Population density	2,130.83	2,149.05	Population per square mile of land area.
Percent male 15-24	14.32	1.97	Percent of population prone to criminal activity (ages 15-24).
Percent black	16.38	14.04	Percent of population that is black or African American (centered and squared).
Crime rate	4,840.99	1,795.54	Number of index crimes divided by county population and multiplied by 100,000.

STEWART J. D'ALESSIO, LISA STOLZENBERG, AND JAMIE L. FLEXON

	Mean	Std. Dev.	Definition
South	.11	.32	Code 1 if county is located in southern state, 0 otherwise.
Community disadvantage	.00	1.00	Factor scores from principal component analysis of 4 variables: (a) % of population (ages 25+) that never graduated from high school, (b) % households with public assistance income, (c) % female-headed households with children, & (d) % unemployed. Larger scores indicate greater community disadvantage.

NOTE: Defendants N=2,323, counties N=35.

6 FINDINGS

We initially begin our analysis by constructing a figure that graphically shows the relationship between the amount of income the police obtain from drug asset forfeiture seizures and the likelihood of a defendant being convicted for a drug offense. Figure 1 shows that there is not much of a visually discernible relationship between drug asset forfeiture income and the probability of being convicted for a felony drug offense. This finding suggests at least tentatively that drug arrests are not more apt to be legally unwarranted in counties where the police derive a greater income from drug asset forfeiture seizures.

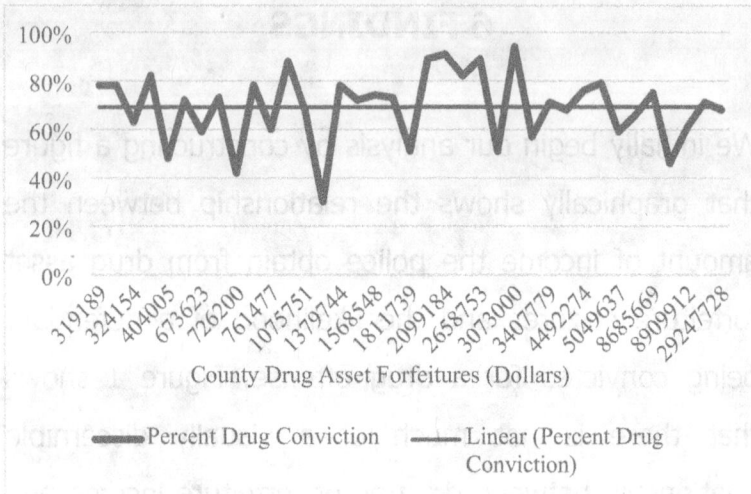

Figure 1. Percent Drug Conviction by the Drug Asset Forfeitures in 37 U.S. Counties

Because the data are multilevel and the dependent variable is a dichotomy, we use a nonlinear hierarchical modeling methodology that uses a penalized quasi-likelihood (PQL) procedure to generate parameter estimates in our multivariate model (Breslow and Clayton, 1993). There are several methodological advantages for using a multilevel model to test the relationship between drug asset forfeiture income and the likelihood of a drug conviction. First, multilevel models avoid violating the assumption of independence among observations because they explicitly recognize the clustering of individuals within higher-level units such as counties.

Second, hierarchical models are advantageous for estimating cross-level effects since all estimates are adjusted for the covariates, regardless of whether they are measured at the individual or contextual level. Finally, hierarchical models not only partition the variance between levels, but they also can statistically separate the variance of the individual-level parameters from sampling variance. The inability to factor out the sampling variance when data are hierarchical results in an underestimate of the explanatory power of contextual variables.

Except for the intercept and the defendant's race variable, we model all the other defendant-level variables as fixed, or constrained to be the same for all the counties since between-county variation in these parameters is not of interest in this study. The intercept and the defendant's race variable are treated as random variables given that we are interested in determining whether variation in drug asset forfeiture income affects the likelihood of conviction for a drug related offense and whether the defendant's race conditions this relationship. The micro-level independent variables were centered by subtracting their grand means, so that the mean of each variable is zero across all cases. This procedure is useful as it tends to attenuate multicollinearity and because it facilitates interpretation of the variable when it becomes the dependent variable in the aggregate-level model. In our case, for example, centering allows the race coefficient to be interpreted as the average gap in conviction between black and white drug defendants. Furthermore, because we permit the intercept and the race variable to vary across counties, we can model any observable differences in the likelihood of conviction with contextual variables. This variability between counties is the outcome to be explained in the between-county models.

The results for the hierarchical generalized linear model are reported in Table 3.[10] A visual inspection of this table reveals that at the defendant-level there are three legal-variables and one extra-legal variable that are statistically noteworthy in the equation. Drug defendants who previously failed to appear in court, who have a second felony charge and who were

---

[10] Population-average estimates with robust standard errors, as described by Zeger et al. (1988), are reported.

detained pretrial have a substantially higher probability of being convicted. In contrast, with the exception of attorney type, the estimated effects of the extra-legal variables included in the equation are small and not of substantive importance. The likelihood of conviction is lower for drug defendants represented by a private attorney after accounting for other factors. The exponentiated value of the attorney type variable is 1.53 (i.e., e .427), which indicates that at the grand centers of all the explanatory variables in the model the odds of conviction for a drug defendant represented by a private attorney are 1.5 times lower than for a drug defendant with a court-appointed attorney. Other research finds that private criminal lawyers are typically more effective than public defenders in representing their clients (Champion, 1989; Hoffman et al., 2005).

Table 3 also shows the results for the effects of the macro-level variables on the likelihood of drug conviction differential and on the black-white drug conviction differential. Our findings reveal a non-consequential effect of the drug asset forfeiture income variable on the likelihood of drug conviction.

The small and non-statistically significant effect of the drug asset forfeiture income variable in the model can be interpreted as evidence against the frequently articulated position that drug asset forfeiture laws are motivating the police to make legally questionable drug arrests. If drug asset forfeiture laws are encouraging the police to generate income, there is a natural expectation of a lower likelihood of conviction in counties where the police derive a higher income from drug asset forfeiture seizures.

Despite this null finding, several aggregate variables show some predictive power in the model. As the likelihood of conviction for nondrug offenses rises, a criminal defendant is more apt to be convicted for a drug offense. Population density has a strong negative effect on the likelihood of conviction. As population density rises in a county, drug defendants are less apt to be convicted. The likelihood of drug conviction is also substantially lower in counties located in southern states. This finding is interesting because while some prior research suggests that criminal justice outcomes tend to be more severe in the south, research that has analyzed data drawn from the SCPS finds that southern counties tend to be less punitive in meting out criminal punishment (Weidner et al., 2004). Finally, results show a statistically discernible nonlinear relationship between racial threat and the likelihood of a drug conviction. The effect of the black population variable is negative and the effect of its squared term is positive on the likelihood of conviction differential. These findings indicate that a U-shaped relationship exists between racial threat and the probability of a drug conviction. When the black population is small in a county, the probability of a drug conviction occurring is high. The likelihood of conviction is also high when the black population is large. However, when the black population is at a moderate level in a county, the likelihood of conviction for a drug related offense is at its lowest. These findings fail to furnish empirical support for Blalock's power-threat hypothesis.

The results for the black-white drug conviction differential are also reported in Table 3. A visual inspection of this model reveals that there fails to be a consequential effect of the drug asset forfeiture income variable on the likelihood that a black felony drug defendant is convicted. The lack of a moderating effect of the drug asset forfeiture income variable on the likelihood of conviction for black drug defendants also fails to support the position that law enforcement's targeting of black citizens for drugs is legally unwarranted. Concerning the other aggregate-level variables, only percent non-convictions and the county of prosecution being located in a southern state, show some predictive power in the model. As the percent of non-drug convictions rises, black felony drug defendants are less apt to be convicted. Black felony drug defendants also have a higher probability of conviction in counties located in southern states.[11]

Table 3. Hierarchical Generalized Linear Models Estimating the Probability of Drug Conviction

Outcome Predictor	Coefficient	Standard Error
Drug conviction probability differential		
Intercept	1.505	.095
Drug forfeitures (ln)	.038	.083
Percent non-drug convictions	.038***	.008
Population density	-.161e-3**	.059e-3
Percent male 15-24	-.005	.040
Percent black	-.069*	.029
Percent black (squared)	.002**	.001

[11] We calculated variance inflation factors (VIF) for all variables included in the estimated models. Serious collinearity problems do not occur when VIFs are less than 10 (Gujarati, 1995). Because all the VIFs were below 4, excessive multicollinearity does not appear to be impacting our results adversely.

Outcome Predictor	Coefficient	Standard Error
Crime rate	.163e-3	.104e-3
South	-1.624***	.338
Community disadvantage	-.027	.115
Black-white drug conviction differential		
Intercept	.070	.128
Drug forfeitures (ln)	.167	.124
Percent non-drug convictions	-.026*	.011
Population density	.113e-3	.090e-3
Percent male 15-24	.071	.051
Percent black	.040	.039
Percent black (squared)	-.002	.001
Crime rate	.124e-3	.114e-3
South	1.739*	.684
Community disadvantage	-.219	.196
Defendant male	-.012	.146
Active CJ status	.049	.120
Court-appointed attorney	.427**	.148
Prior FTA	.321**	.120
Second felony charge	.472*	.197
No. of charges	.029	.036
Pretrial incarceration	.521*	.243
Defendant's age	.005	.025
Defendant's age (squared)	-.123e-3	.342e-3
Drug sale	.604	.379
Criminal record	.120	.070

NOTE: Results are estimated from population-average models with robust standard errors.
*p < .05, **p < .01, ***p < .01 (two-tailed tests).

7 DISCUSSION AND CONCLUSION

Well-meaning purposive social action initiated by the government often has unintended and detrimental effects for society (Merton, 1936). The criminal justice system is replete with examples of goal displacement whereby the publicly espoused and often abstractly defined goals of a criminal justice agency are superseded by the more immediate, easily quantifiable and self-serving objectives of organizational exigencies (Rothman, 2002). Although the primary intent of drug asset forfeiture laws is to decrease crime, many remain convinced that the organizational imperative to generate income is having a corrupting influence by fostering a culture of greed among the police. Yet one has to recognize that by simply showing that the police are directing their efforts on drug enforcement is by no means sinister. Even a casual observer might easily draw the conclusion that the focus on drug enforcement, even with the monetary incentive provided by the government, is a legitimate and worthwhile endeavor for the police because the trafficking and consumption of illegal drugs is correlated strongly with crime and violence.

We initially theorized that if drug asset forfeiture laws are having an adverse influence on the police in the performance of their drug enforcement duties, then the police are probably making unwarranted drug arrests in an attempt to seize the cash and property of citizens. We speculated that as the amount of income the police derive from drug asset forfeiture seizures rises, the likelihood of conviction for a drug related felony offense should decrease because the lure of money will motivate the police to make drug arrests that are legally questionable. We also thought that black drug defendants might have a lower probability of conviction in counties where police derive a greater amount of income from drug asset forfeiture seizures.

Results from a multilevel analysis showed that the income the police derive from drug asset forfeiture seizures has little influence on a drug defendant's likelihood of conviction. Felony drug defendants being prosecuted in counties where drug asset forfeiture income is high do not have a significantly lower probability of conviction controlling for other factors related to criminal justice processing outcome. This finding suggests that the police are not making unwarranted drug arrests, as determined by the court system, in order to generate supplemental income. Results also show that the race of the defendant fails to moderate the relationship between the amount of income derived from drug asset forfeiture seizures and the likelihood of a drug conviction. As the amount of income the police obtain from drug asset forfeiture seizures grows, black drug defendants are no more likely than are white drug defendants to be convicted. There is also no evidence of racial disparity in the likelihood of a drug conviction generally. This finding has relevance in regards to whether the police are performing their drug enforcement duties in a racially biased manner.

Although our legal system's claim to legitimacy is dependent on the public's perception of fairness and equity in the decision to arrest, debate persist as to whether the police are racially discriminatory when enforcing drug laws. Evidence supporting this view comes from the observation that blacks are arrested for drugs in numbers far out of proportion to their numbers in the general population, especially for less dangerous types of drugs such as marijuana where the black arrest rate for marijuana possession in 2010 was 716 per 100,000 as compared to 192 per 100,000 for whites (American Civil Liberties Union, 2013).

Although it is readily acknowledged that blacks are arrested for marijuana possession in numbers far out of proportion to their numbers in the general population, disagreement remains as to what this situation exactly means. Some maintain that racial disparity in arrests for marijuana possession is the result of racially biased drug enforcement practices. Black citizens face a higher probability of arrest for marijuana possession because the police view them as having a greater proclivity than whites to use and sell drugs. Such a negative stereotype is thought to compel police to monitor and arrest blacks more frequently for marijuana possession than warranted based on their actual usage patterns.

The American Civil Liberties Union (2013) recently published a study advancing the position that the police are racially biased in their use of the arrest sanction for marijuana possession. Despite the fact that surveys of the general population show that black and white citizens report similar usage rates of marijuana (Substance Abuse and Mental Health Services Administration, 2011), the American Civil Liberties Union (ACLU) reports that on average a black person is 3.73 times more likely than a white person to be arrested for marijuana possession. As the ACLU (2013:66) writes:

> *Despite the pronounced disparities in arrest rates of whites and Blacks for marijuana possession, rates of marijuana use and non-use between whites and Blacks are roughly equal. Therefore, the wide racial disparities in marijuana possession arrest rates cannot be explained by differences in marijuana usage rates between whites and Blacks.*

However, there are a couple of problems with the ACLU's analysis. One problem relates to what is referred to as sample selection bias (Berk, 1983). The ACLU proffers that because marijuana use among black and whites in the general population is similar, then black and whites should have comparable arrest rates for marijuana possession. However, large national surveys like the National Household Survey on Drug Abuse tend to undercount chronic criminal offenders (Cernkovich et al., 1985). Since research finds that blacks are more apt than whites to be chronic criminal offenders (Elliott and Ageton, 1980; Piper, 1985) and because individuals who interact with criminal justice system consume the vast majority of drugs in this country (Rhodes and McDonald, 1991), it seems highly probable that large national drug use surveys underestimate marijuana use among black citizens by undercounting those black citizens most likely to use marijuana and other types of drugs. These undercounted individuals are also much more inclined than the people queried in these types of surveys to come into contact with the police.

A second problem with the ACLU's analysis is that the self-report data pertaining to an individual's marijuana use, and other illegal behaviors for that matter, are likely subject to response bias because of a respondent's hesitancy in reporting socially unacceptable behaviors. The underreporting of marijuana use by survey respondents is not a serious problem if whites and blacks underreport their marijuana use at the same rate. However, given that disparaging labels related to drug use are often used to depict blacks in our society (Gibbs, 1988), the negative stereotype of black citizens of having an enhanced propensity to use illegal drugs might compel them more than whites to give socially acceptable answers in surveys (Steele, 1997). This situation in turn would result in an increase in their underreporting of marijuana use.

Although it is difficult to determine whether respondents in large national surveys are giving truthful answers regarding their illegal drug use, it is possible to make such a determination by analyzing data collected from the Arrestee Drug Abuse Monitoring (ADAM) Program.[12] The ADAM program samples male arrestees who are brought into booking facilities (jails) in a number of heavily populated counties across the United States.[13] These arrestees are interviewed about their drug use and are asked to provide urine specimens. Respondents are assured of anonymity. More than 90 percent of the arrestees who are approached for interviews comply, while 85 percent of them agree to furnish urine specimens.

---

[12] ADAM II, 2009. Annual Report: Arrestee Drug Abuse Monitoring Program II. Office of National Drug Control Policy, Executive Office of the President. Washington, DC. June 2010.

[13] Professor Stolzenberg was the former Site-Director and Professor D'Alessio the former Site-Coordinator for Miami-Dade County's Arrestee Drug Abuse Monitoring (ADAM) Program, which was funded by the National Institute of Justice.

Interviews usually occur within 48 hours after arrest in most sites. Refusal rates have been found not to differ by arrestees' ethnicity, age, employment, or charge (Chaiken and Chaiken, 1992). The interview can usually be administered in about 20 minutes, and the instrument consists of items that measure drug use history, patterns of use, and demographic information such as the race/ethnicity of the arrestee. Urine specimens are collected immediately following the interview and tests for drug screening are conducted off-site. These screening tests can generally detect the use of marijuana within the 30 days prior to the individual's arrest.

Using data drawn from the ADAM Program for 2009, we undertook an analysis to determine the extent of the potential undercounting and underreporting problems that vitiate the study conducted by the ACLU.[14] If the ACLU's claim that marijuana use is similar for blacks and whites in the general population is accurate, then there should be

---

[14] In 2009, ADAM data collection occurred in the following 10 U.S. counties: Atlanta, GA, Charlotte, NC, Chicago, IL, Denver, CO, Indianapolis, IN, Minneapolis, MN, New York, NY, Portland, OR, Sacramento, CA, and Washington, DC.

little difference in the results of urine tests for marijuana use among black and white arrestees. Furthermore, because white and black arrestees are queried in an interview about their drug use immediately prior to being drug tested, a statistical comparison can be made between black and white arrestees in regards to whether one racial group is more likely than the other group to underreport their marijuana use.

Table 4 reports the results for self-reported marijuana use and for the urine tests for marijuana use. A distinction is made in the table between all arrestees and arrestees for non-drug offenses because of the overrepresentation of black citizens being arrested for drugs. Hispanic arrestees are excluded from the data depicted in the table. Despite the fact that national surveys such as the National Household Survey on Drug Abuse show similar rates of marijuana use among blacks and whites in the general population, the results depicted in Table 4 clearly show that marijuana use is much higher among black arrestees than among white arrestees. The likelihood of testing positive for marijuana use is 9.5 percent higher for black arrestees generally and 9.4 percent higher for black non-drug arrestees, as compared to white arrestees. These racial differences are statistically noteworthy and are unlikely to have occurred by chance alone.

A visual inspection of Table 4 also shows that there is a racial difference in the underreporting of marijuana use. Although both white and black arrestees underreport their marijuana use, black arrestees are 6.7 percent more likely than white arrestees to underreport their use of marijuana. A substantive racial difference in the underreporting of marijuana use is also observed for non-drug arrestees. Our results are buttressed by previous research using the ADAM data that also found that black arrestees are much more inclined than white arrestees to underreport their drug use as determined by a urine test (Harrell, 1997).

The data presented in Table 4 cast doubt on the ACLU's assertion that because blacks and whites use marijuana at similar rates, the racial disparity in marijuana procession arrests must be wholly due to racially biased law enforcement practices. Based on the urine tests of arrestees booked into jails across the U.S., we find that black arrestees are significantly more likely than white arrestees to use marijuana. In sum, when one considers the results presented in Table 3 and the findings generated in the analysis of the ADAM data, it appears that the police are enforcing the drug laws in a racially unbiased manner and that the racial disparity in drug arrests most likely reflects greater use of illegal drugs among black citizens.[15]

---

[15] Other research also shows that the disproportionately high arrest rate for black citizens for crimes such as robbery and assault is most likely attributable to differential involvement rather than to racially biased law enforcement practices. Using data from the National Incident-Based Reporting System (NIBRS), D'Alessio and Stolzenberg (2003) assessed the effect of an offender's race on the probability of arrest for 335,619 incidents of forcible rape, robbery, aggravated assault and simple assault. They restricted their study to these four offenses because it is in these types of crimes that the victim is confronted by the criminal offender and hence is able to get some indication of the offender's race and other demographic characteristics. The baseline model for their comparisons was the equiprobability hypothesis that relative to violation frequency as reported by crime victims, the likelihood of arrest for white and black offenders would be roughly equal. Their multivariate logistic regression results showed that the odds of arrest for white offenders was approximately 22 percent higher for robbery, 13 percent higher for aggravated assault, and 9 percent higher for simple assault than they were for black offenders. The race of the offender played no noteworthy role in the likelihood of arrest for the crime of forcible rape.

Table 4. Marijuana Use among White and Black Male Arrestees

	White	Black	2 sample t-test
All arrestees			
% reported use in past week	39.6	42.4	1.755
	(1,589)	(2,522)	
% tested positive	44.4	53.9	5.582***
	(1,401)	(2,248)	
2 sample t-test	2.655**	7.937***	
Non-drug arrestees			
% reported use in past week	37.1	39.2	1.232
	(1,337)	(2,082)	
% tested positive	41.9	51.3	5.046***
	(1,173)	(1,856)	
2 sample t-test	2.456**	7.620***	

SOURCE: ADAM II, 2009. Annual Report, Arrestee Drug Abuse Monitoring Pro-gram II. Office of National Drug Control Policy, Executive Office of the Presi-dent. Washington, DC. June 2010.
*P < .05, **P < .01, *** P < .001.

In conclusion, the results evinced in this study have noteworthy implications for drug policy. The findings reported here suggest that the police are not being overly influenced by the desire to generate supplemental income, but rather are focusing their attention on drug enforcement owning to the strong nexus reported between illegal drugs and violence. Nonetheless, future research should investigate the effect of drug asset forfeiture income on the outcomes in civil forfeiture proceedings since the state can also use these types of proceedings to seize an individual's cash and property. In a civil forfeiture proceeding criminal charges need not be filed against the defendant, the standard of proof necessary to seize a person's property is lower and less constitutional rights are afforded the defendant (Rosenberg, 1988). Thus, despite the null findings reported here, it is still plausible that the amount of income that the police derive from drug asset forfeiture seizures influences the outcome in civil drug forfeiture cases. This topic certainly warrants additional research.

8 REFERENCES

Albonetti, Celesta A. 1987. Prosecutorial discretion: The effects of uncertainty. *Law & Society Review* 21:291-313.

Alexander, Michelle. 2012. *The New Jim Crow: Mass Incarceration in the Age of Colorblindness*. New York: New Press.

Angus Reid Public Opinion. 2012. *Americans Decry War on Drugs, Support Legalizing Marijuana*. Vancouver, BC: Angus Reid Public Opinion.

American Civil Liberties Union. 2013. *The War on Marijuana in Black and White: Billions of Dollars Wasted on Racially Biased Arrests*. New York, American Civil Liberties Union.

Baicker, Katherine and Mireille Jacobson. 2007. Finders keepers: Forfeiture laws, policing incentives, and local budgets. *Journal of Public Economics* 91:2113-36.

Beckett, Katherine, Kris Nyrop, Lori Pfingst, and Melissa Bowen. 2005. Drug use, drug possession arrests, and the question of race: Lessons from Seattle. *Social Problems* 52:419-41.

Berk, Richard A. 1983. An introduction to sample selection bias in sociological data. *American Sociological Review* 48:386-98.

Blalock, Hubert M. Jr. 1967. *Toward a Theory of Minority-Group Relations*. New York: Capricorn Books.

Blumenson, Eric and Eva S. Nilsen. 1998. Policing for profit: The drug war's hidden economic agenda. *University of Chicago Law Review* 65:35-114.

Boland, Barbara. 1983. *The Prosecution of Felony Arrests*. Washington, DC: Bureau of Justice Statistics.

Breslow, N.E. and D. G. Clayton. 1993. Approximate inference in generalized linear mixed models. *Journal of the American Statistical Association* 88:9-25.

Bureau of Justice Statistics. 2007. *State Court Processing Statistics, 1990-2004: Felony Defendants in Large Urban Counties*. Washington, DC: Department of Justice.

Burkhart, W. Robert, Shirley Melnicoe, Annesley K. Schmidt, Linda J. McKay, and Cheryl Martorana. 1982. *The Effects of the Exclusionary Rule: A Study in California*. Washington, DC: National Institute of Justice.

Carpenter, Dick M. II and Lee McGrath. 2013. *Rotten Reporting in the Peach State: Civil Forfeiture in Georgia Leaves the Public in the Dark*. Arlington, VA: Institute for Justice.

Cassella, Stefan D. 2008. The case for civil forfeiture: Why in Rem proceedings are an essential tool for recovering the proceeds of crime. *Journal of Money Laundering Control* 11:8-14.

Cassella, Stefan D. 2013. *Civil Asset Recovery: The American Experience*. Working Title. Oxford University Press.

Cernkovich, Stephen A., Peggy C. Giordano and Meredith D. Pugh. 1985. Chronic offenders: The missing cases in self-report delinquency research. *Journal of Criminal Law and Criminology* 76:705-32.

Chaiken, Jonathan P. and Marcia Chaiken. 1992. *Analysis of the Drug Use Forecasting (DUF) Sample of Adult Arrestees*. Draft Report to the National Institute of Justice. Washington, DC: Abt Associates.

Chambliss, William J. and Robert J. Seidman. 1971. *Law, Order and Power*. Reading, MA: Addison-Wesley.

Champion, Dean J. 1989. Private counsels and

public defenders: Look at weak cases, prior records and leniency in bargaining. *Journal of Criminal Justice* 17:253-63.

Coe, Charles K. and Deborah Lamm Wiesel. 2001. Police budgeting: Winning strategies. *Public Administration Review* 61:718-27.

D'Alessio, Stewart J. and Lisa Stolzenberg. 2003. Race and the probability of arrest. *Social Forces* 81:1383-99.

Degenhardt, Louisa and Wayne Hall. 2012. Extent of illicit drug use and dependence, and their contribution to the global burden of disease. *The Lancet* 379:55-70.

Downs, Anthony. 1967. *Inside Bureaucracy*. Boston: Little, Brown & Company.

Drug Policy Alliance. 2013. *Drug War Statistics*. New York: Drug Policy Alliance.

See http://www.drugpolicy.org/drug-war.

Edgeworth, Dee R. 2009. *Asset Forfeiture: Practice and Procedure in State and Federal Courts, 2nd Edition*. Chicago: American Bar Association.

Eisenstein, James, Roy B. Flemming and Peter F. Nardulli. 1999. *The Contours of Justice: Communities and their Courts*. Lanham, Maryland: University Press of America.

Eitle, David, Stewart J. D'Alessio and Lisa Stolzenberg. 2002. Racial threat and social control: A test of the political, economic, and threat of black crime hypotheses. *Social Forces* 81:557-76.

Eitle, David, Lisa Stolzenberg and Stewart J. D'Alessio. 2005. Police organizational factors, the racial composition of the police, and the probability of arrest. *Justice Quarterly* 22:30-57.

Elliott, Delbert S. and Suzanne S. Ageton. 1980. Reconciling race and class differences in self-reported and official estimates of delinquency. *American Sociological Review* 45:95-110.

Finneran, Richard E. and Steven K. Luther. 2013. Criminal forfeiture and the Sixth Amendment: The role of the jury at common law. *Cardozo Law Review* 35:1-77.

Gibbs, Jewelle. 1988. *Young, Black, and Male in America*. New York: Auburn House.

Goode, Erich. 2002. Drug arrests at the millennium. *Social Science and Public Policy* 39:41-45.

Gross, John P. 2013. Too poor to hire a lawyer but

not indigent: How states use the federal poverty guidelines to deprive defendants of their Sixth Amendment right to counsel. *Washington and Lee Law Review* 70:1173-1219.

Grosskopf, S., K. Hayes and J. Hirschberg. 1995. Fiscal stress and the production of public safety: A distance function approach. *Journal of Public Economics* 57:277-96.

Gujarati, Damodar N. 1995. *Basic Econometrics*, 3rd edition. New York: McGraw-Hill.

Harrell, Adele V. 1997. The validity of self-reported drug use data: The accuracy of responses on confidential self-administered answered sheets. *NIDA Research Monograph* 167:37-58.

Hoffman, Morris B., Paul H. Rubin and Joanna M. Shepherd. 2005. An empirical study of public defender effectiveness: Self-selection by the "marginally indigent." *Ohio State Journal of Criminal Law* 3:223-55.

Human Rights Watch. 2009. *Decades of Disparity: Drug Arrests and Race in the United States*. New York: Human Rights Watch.

Johnson, Derek and Thomas J. Miceli. 2013. *Asset*

Forfeiture and Criminal Deterrence. University of Connecticut: Working paper.

Kim, Douglas. 1997. Asset forfeiture: Giving up your constitutional rights. *Campbell Law Review* 19:527-78:

King, Ryan S. 2008. *Disparity by Geography: The War on Drugs in America's Cities.* Washington, DC: The Sentencing Project.

Lemos, Margaret H. and Max Minzner. 2014. For-profit public enforcement. *Harvard Law Review* 127:853-913.

Levinson, Daryl J. 2005. Empire-building government in constitutional law. *Harvard Law Review* 118:915-72.

Lynskeya, Michael T. and John Stranga. 2013. The global burden of drug use and mental disorders. *The Lancet* 382:1540-42.

Mast, Brent D., Bruce L. Benson and David W. Rasmussen. 2000. Entrepreneurial police and drug enforcement policy. *Public Choice* 104:285-308.

Merton, Robert K. 1936. The unanticipated consequences of purposive social action. *American Sociological Review* 1:894-904.

Moore, Mark H. 1990. Supply reduction and drug law enforcement. Pp. 109-57 in *Crime and Justice: A Review of Research*, Vol. 13, Drugs and Crime, edited by Michael Tonry and James Q. Wilson.

National Drug Intelligence Center. 2011. *The Economic Impact of Illicit Drug Use on American Society*. Washington DC: U.S. Department of Justice.

Niskanen, William A. 1991. A Reflection on Bureaucracy and Representative Government. Pages 13-31 in *The Budget-Maximizing Bureaucrat: Appraisals and Evidence*, edited by Andre Blais and Stephanie Dion. Pittsburgh: PA: University of Pittsburgh Press.

Piper, Elizabeth S. 1985. Violent recidivism and chronicity in the 1958 Philadelphia cohort. *Journal of Quantitative Criminology* 1:319-44.

Rhodes, William and Douglas C. McDonald. 1991. *What America's Users Spend on Illegal Drugs*. An Office of the National Drug Control Policy (Tech. Rep.).Washington, DC: U.S. Government Printing Office.

Robinson, Matthew B. and Renee G. Scherlen. 2007. *Lies, Damned Lies, and Drug War Statistics: A*

Critical Analysis of Claims Made by the Office of National Drug Control Policy. Albany: State University of New York Press.

Rosenberg, Jay A. 1988. Constitutional rights and civil forfeiture actions. *Columbia Law Review* 88:390-406.

Rothman, David J. 2002. *Conscience and Convenience: The Asylum and Its Alternatives in Progressive America*, 2nd edition. New Jersey: Aldine Transaction.

Sabol, William J., Heather Couture and Paige M. Harrison. 2007. *Prisoners in 2006*. Washington, DC: Bureau of Justice Statistics.

Saxe, Leonard, Charles Kadushin, Andrew Beveridge, David Livert, Elizabeth Tighe, David Rindskopf, Julie Ford, and Archie Brodsky. 2001. The visibility of illicit drugs: Implications for community-based drug control strategies. *American Journal of Public Health* 91:1987-94.

Schneider, Andrew and Mary P. Flaherty. 1991. *Government Seizures Victimize Innocent*. Pittsburgh Press, August 11, 1991, at Al.

Steele, Claude M. 1997. A threat in the air: How

stereotypes shape intellectual identity and performance. *American Psychologist* 52:613-29.

Stellwagen, Lindsey D and Wylie, Kimberly A. 1985. *Strategies for Supplementing the Police Budget*. Washington, DC: US National Institute of Justice.

Stolzenberg, Lisa and Stewart J. D'Alessio. 2003. A multilevel analysis of the effect of cocaine price on cocaine use among arrestees. *Journal of Criminal Justice* 31:185-95.

Stolzenberg, Lisa, Stewart J. D'Alessio and David Eitle. 2013. Race and cumulative discrimination in the prosecution of criminal defendants. *Race and Justice* 3:275-99.

Substance Abuse and Mental Health Services Administration. 2011. *Results from the 2010 National Survey on Drug Use and Health: Summary of National Findings*. NSDUH Series H-41, HHS Publication No. No. SMA 11-4658. Rockville, MD: Substance Abuse and Mental Health Services Administration.

Substance Abuse and Mental Health Services Administration. 2012. *Results from the 2011 National Survey on Drug Use and Health: Summary of National Findings*. NSDUH Series H-44, HHS Publication No.

SMA 12-4713. Rockville, MD: Substance Abuse and Mental Health Services Administration.

Vera Institute of Justice. 1981. *Felony Arrests: Their Prosecution and Disposition in New York City's Courts*. New York: Longman.

Vigorita, Michael S. 2001. Prior offense type and the probability of incarceration: The importance of current offense type and sentencing jurisdiction. *Journal of Contemporary Criminal Justice* 17:167-93.

Weber, Max. 1978. Economy and Society. Edited and translated by Guenther Roth and Claus Wittich, Vol. 2. Berkeley, CA: University of California Press.

Weidner, Robert R., Richard Frase and Iain Pardoe. 2004. Explaining sentence severity in large urban counties: A multilevel analysis of contextual and case-level factors. *Prison Journal* 4:184-207.

Williams, Marian R. 2002. Civil asset forfeiture: Where does the money go? *Criminal Justice Review* 27: 321-29.

Zeger, Scott L., Kung-Yee Liang, and Paul S. Albert. 1988. Models for longitudinal data: A likelihood approach. *Biometrics* 44:1049-60.

ABOUT THE AUTHORS

Lisa Stolzenberg is a professor and chair of the Department of Criminology and Criminal Justice at Florida International University's Steven J. Green School of International and Public Affairs. She is also president of We Love Animals Rescue, Inc., a 501(c)(3) public charity located in Hollywood, Florida. She has a BA in criminal justice from the University of Florida and an MS and PhD in criminology from Florida State University.

Stewart J. D'Alessio is a professor in the Department of Criminology and Criminal Justice at Florida International University's Steven J. Green School of International and Public Affairs. He previously served as a captain in the Military Police Corps and participated in Operation Just Cause and Operation Desert Storm. He has a BA in history from Stetson University and an MS and PhD in criminology from Florida State University.

Jamie L. Flexon is an associate professor in the Department of Criminology and Criminal Justice at Florida International University's Steven J. Green

School of International and Public Affairs. Her research interests include juvenile delinquency, juvenile psychopathy, criminal justice issues related to punishment, and policy evaluation. She has a BA, MA and PhD in criminal justice from the University at Albany, State University of New York.